People in Our Government

Representative

Linda Hopkins

LIGHTBOX
openlightbox.com

LIGHTBOX

Go to
www.openlightbox.com
and enter this book's
unique code.

ACCESS CODE

LBXD3868

Lightbox is an all-inclusive digital solution for the teaching and learning of curriculum topics in an original, groundbreaking way. Lightbox is based on National Curriculum Standards.

STANDARD FEATURES OF LIGHTBOX

AUDIO High-quality narration using text-to-speech system

ACTIVITIES Printable PDFs that can be emailed and graded

SLIDESHOWS Pictorial overviews of key concepts

VIDEOS Embedded high-definition video clips

WEBLINKS Curated links to external, child-safe resources

TRANSPARENCIES Step-by-step layering of maps, diagrams, charts, and timelines

INTERACTIVE MAPS Interactive maps and aerial satellite imagery

QUIZZES Ten multiple choice questions that are automatically graded and emailed for teacher assessment

KEY WORDS Matching key concepts to their definitions

Representative

Contents

What Is a Representative?

A representative is someone who serves in the United States House of Representatives. The House of Representatives is one of two houses in the U.S. Congress. The other house is called the **Senate**. Representatives are also called congressmen or congresswomen.

James Madison was one of the very first congressmen. He helped write the U.S. **Constitution**. Madison also proposed the first 10 **amendments** to the Constitution. These amendments were called the Bill of Rights. Madison became known as the Father of the Constitution.

After serving four terms as a representative, James Madison became president of the United States in 1808.

The Government

The U.S. government is made up of three branches. Each branch has its own role. Together, they take care of the country and its people.

The legislative branch makes the country's laws. The executive branch carries out the laws. The judicial branch settles any problems with the country's laws. The House of Representatives is part of the legislative branch.

The legislative branch does most of its work at the U.S. Capitol in Washington, D.C.

Structure of the U.S. Government

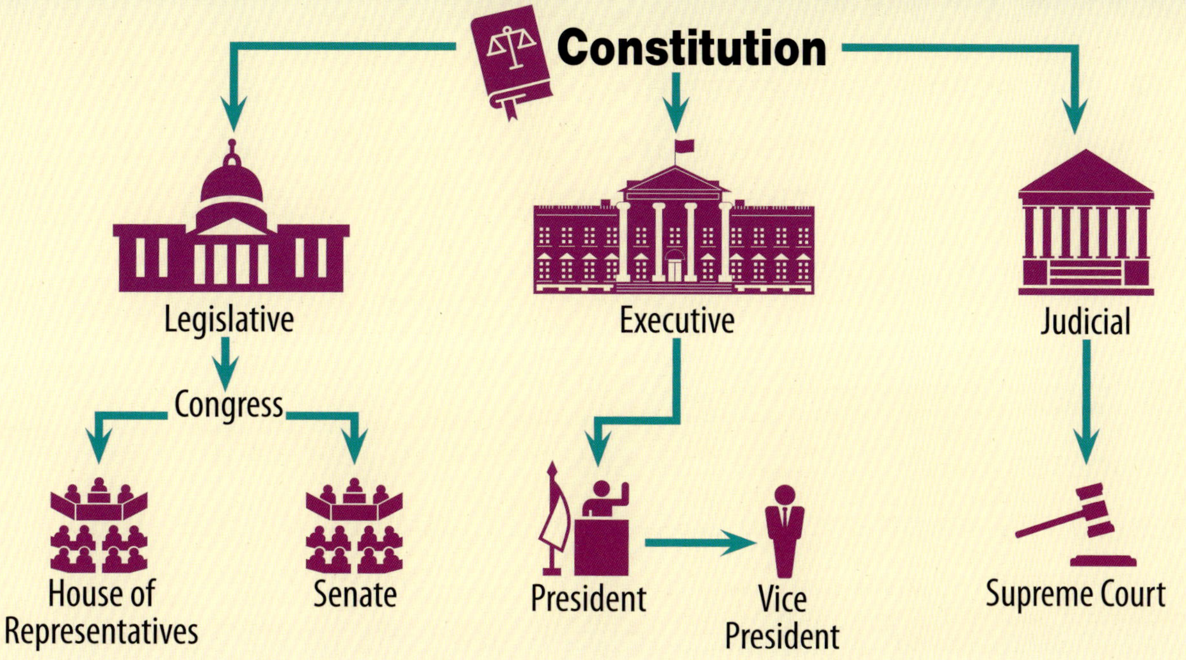

The Role

A representative serves the people in one of a state's districts. Districts are areas of each state that have equal populations. The United States is divided into 435 districts. This means there are 435 representatives. Representatives serve their **constituents** by introducing bills that can become the country's laws.

Representative Barbara Comstock introduced a bill called the Inspiring the Next Space Pioneers, Innovators, Researchers, and Explorers (INSPIRE) Women Act. This bill instructs **NASA** to encourage more girls to study science. It became law in 2017.

Barbara Comstock's INSPIRE Women Act required NASA to make a plan for how current astronauts can work with students.

In 1983, Sally Ride became the first woman from the United States to go into space. Since then, more than 40 U.S. women have also made the journey.

Each representative's district has approximately **710,000 people.**

Barbara Comstock was a representative for Virginia from **2015** to **2018.**

Representative Alexandria Ocasio-Cortez works on issues relating to women's rights and protecting the environment.

What It Takes

A person must meet certain rules to become a representative. He or she must be at least 25 years old, must have been a **citizen** of the United States for at least seven years, and must live in the state he or she represents. The founders of the United States wanted representatives to closely resemble the people in their district.

In 2018, Alexandria Ocasio-Cortez became the youngest woman ever to be **elected** to the House of Representatives. She was 29 years old. Ocasio-Cortez represents New York's 14th District, which covers part of New York City.

New York State has 27 districts. Twelve of them are in New York City.

Getting the Job

Representatives are elected every two years, and they can be reelected an unlimited number of times. Anyone who meets the rules to become a representative can start a **campaign** for the job. It takes work to be elected as a representative.

1 A person who wants to be elected as a representative must raise at least $5,000. He or she is then recognized as a **candidate**.

2 After the money is raised, the candidate has 10 days to set up a campaign **committee**. He or she must also fill out and submit forms.

3

The candidate travels around his or her district to meet people. He or she lets them know how he or she will serve the district and make it a better place to live.

4

On Election Day, people go to the polls to vote for the person they want as their representative.

5

The person with the most votes wins the election and becomes the representative.

The Capitol

The U.S. Capitol is located at the end of the National Mall. The U.S. Congress has met there since 1800. Representatives and senators all have offices in the building.

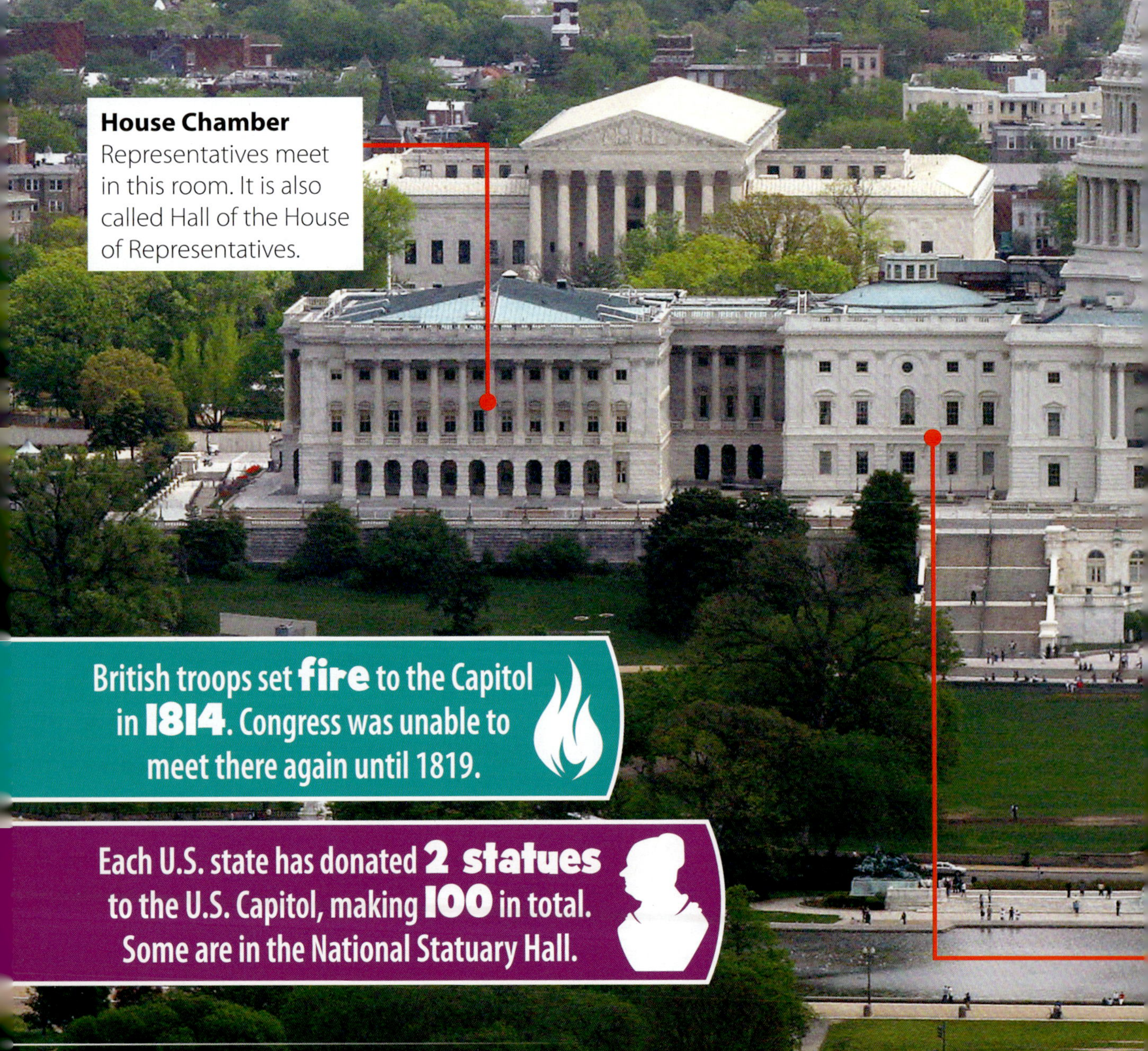

House Chamber
Representatives meet in this room. It is also called Hall of the House of Representatives.

British troops set **fire** to the Capitol in **1814**. Congress was unable to meet there again until 1819.

Each U.S. state has donated **2 statues** to the U.S. Capitol, making **100** in total. Some are in the National Statuary Hall.

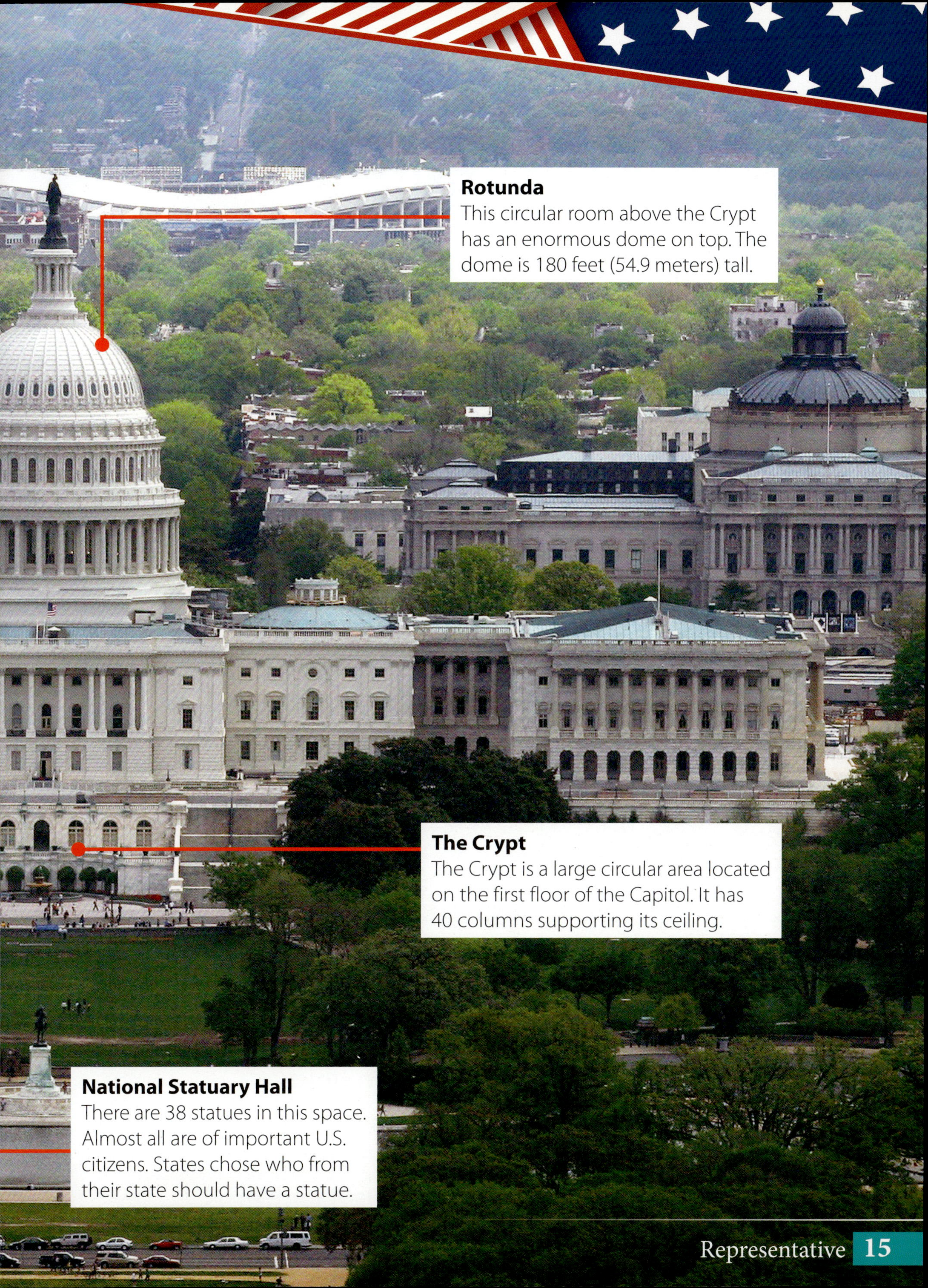

Rotunda

This circular room above the Crypt has an enormous dome on top. The dome is 180 feet (54.9 meters) tall.

The Crypt

The Crypt is a large circular area located on the first floor of the Capitol. It has 40 columns supporting its ceiling.

National Statuary Hall

There are 38 statues in this space. Almost all are of important U.S. citizens. States chose who from their state should have a statue.

Leading in Public

People look to their congressmen and congresswomen to represent them in the government. Representatives try to make their constituents' lives better. They do this in a variety of ways.

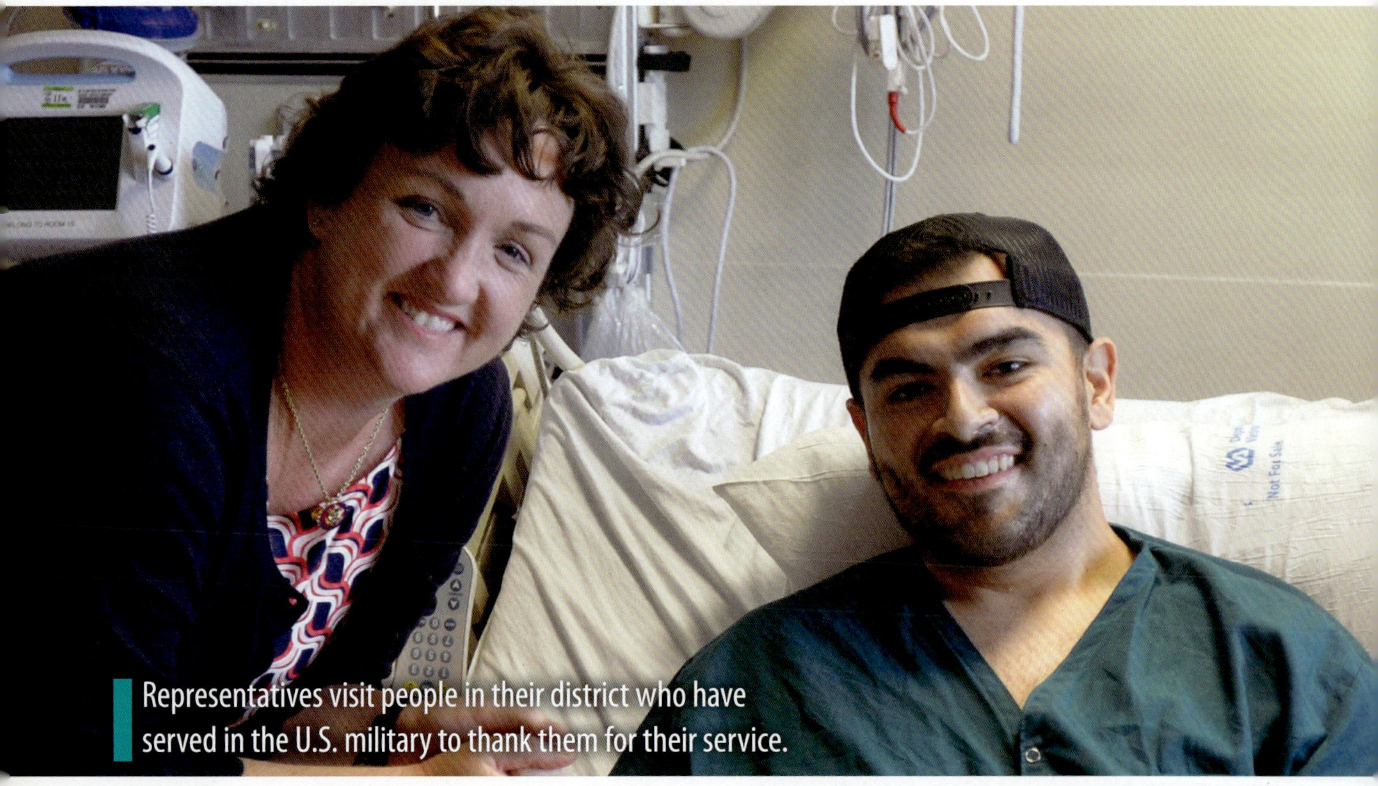

Representatives visit people in their district who have served in the U.S. military to thank them for their service.

Travel Around the District

Representatives travel around their district and meet with constituents. They listen to concerns or issues people are having. They also hold meetings where constituents can ask questions. Representatives take this information and think of new laws that could address people's concerns.

Send Information to Constituents

It is important for representatives to stay in touch with constituents so that the representatives can properly represent constituents' views in the House.

Representatives often send out letters to their constituents to tell them about things happening in the government. They also send emails inviting constituents to upcoming events. These can be town halls, career fairs, or other informational activities.

Constituents sometimes have the opportunity to visit the office of their representative while on a tour of the Capitol.

Lead Tours Around the Capitol

Representatives invite schools and groups from their district to the Capitol. They show these visitors around the building. This gives people the chance to see where their representative works and also what the representative is doing for them there.

Represent the State in the Federal Government

A representative introduces a bill by presenting information about the bill to a committee.

Representatives propose bills that will help their district as well as the whole nation. Bills can be written by one representative or a group of them. Bills have to be passed before they go to the president to become law.

A Day in the Life

Representatives are very busy people, with many things to do. They have meetings with constituents, their fellow representatives, and other people in the government. Their days are full.

Representatives meet with the media to talk about the work they are doing.

8:00 am	The representative meets with his or her staff to discuss the upcoming day.
10:00 am	The representative attends a committee meeting to discuss a proposed bill about gun control.
11:00 am	An eighth grade class visits from the representative's district. He or she gives the students a tour of the Capitol.
12:00 pm	The representative has a lunch meeting with businessmen and businesswomen to get their views on a change in **taxes**.
2:00 pm	The representative talks to the media about a new bill to help the environment.
2:30 pm	The representative attends a session in the House Chamber to debate a new bill with the rest of the representatives.

Notable Representatives

Members of the House are called representatives because they represent the people in their districts. They create bills that they believe will help people. Representatives have had a big impact on the history of the U.S. government.

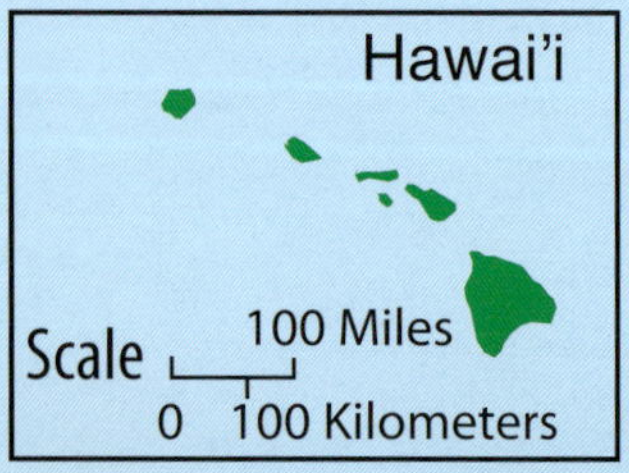

Gabrielle Giffords
Years in Office:
2007–2012

Giffords was a representative for Arizona. She worked on immigration laws and U.S. border security. Giffords was shot while meeting constituents in 2011. She survived but left Congress in 2012 to focus on her recovery.

Henry Clay

Years in Office: 1811–1821, 1823–1825

Clay represented Kentucky. He became the youngest Speaker of the House. This is the leader of the House, who is chosen by the other representatives. Clay also served in the U.S. Senate for more than 15 years.

Adam Clayton Powell

Years in Office: 1945–1967, 1969–1971

Powell was elected to the House of Representatives to represent New York. He served 12 terms. Powell believed in **civil rights** and fought for the rights of African Americans.

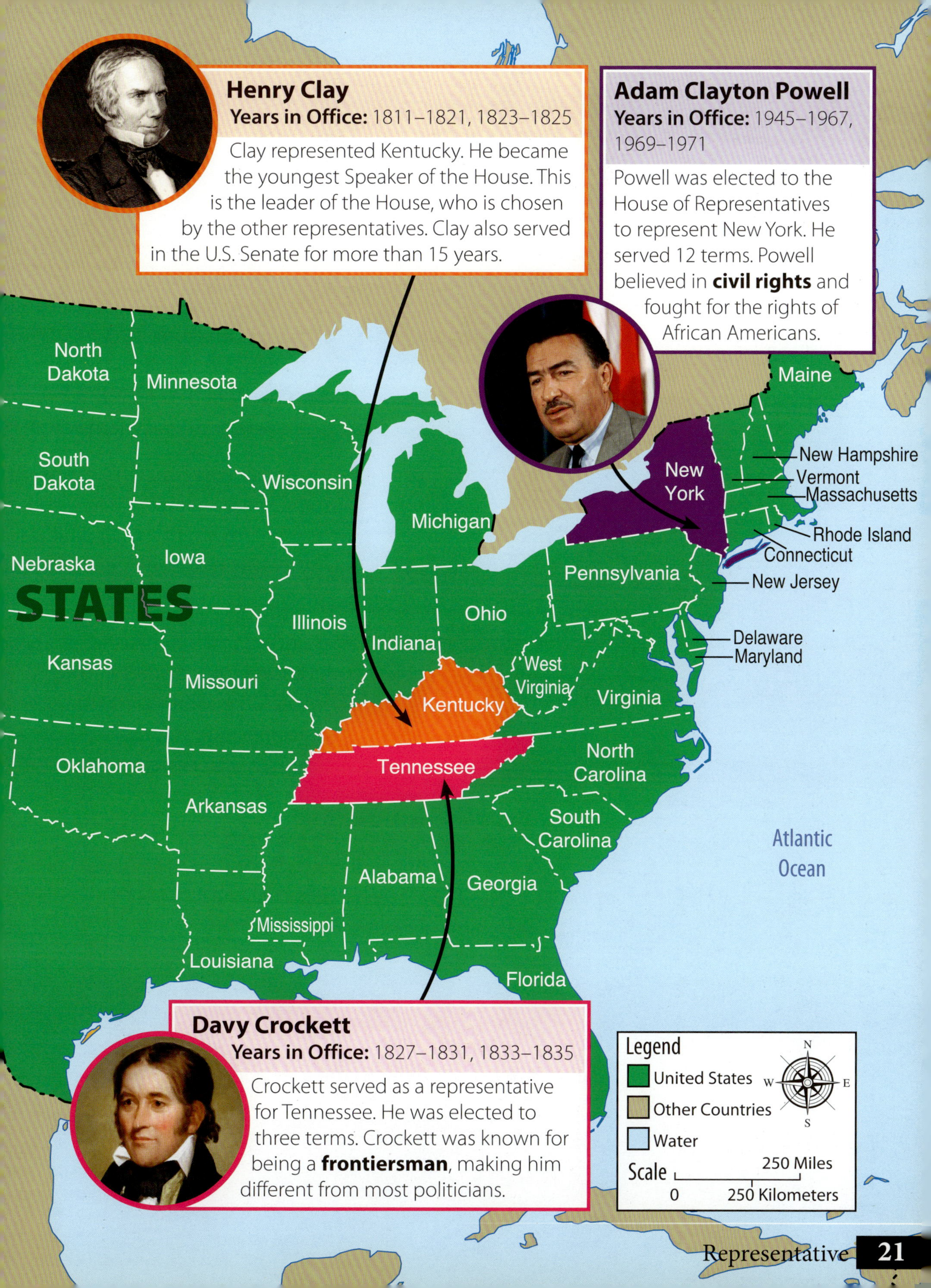

Davy Crockett

Years in Office: 1827–1831, 1833–1835

Crockett served as a representative for Tennessee. He was elected to three terms. Crockett was known for being a **frontiersman**, making him different from most politicians.

Quiz

1 What are representatives also called?

2 How old must someone be to run as a representative?

3 How often are representatives elected?

4 Where does the U.S. Congress meet?

5 How many statues were donated by each state to the U.S. Capitol?

6 Which representative was known for being a frontiersman?

ANSWERS

1 Congressmen and congresswomen **2** At least 25 years old **3** Every two years **4** The Capitol
5 2 **6** Davy Crockett

Key Words

amendments: sections that are added to a law or rule

campaign: an effort to become elected

candidate: a person who seeks or is put forward for a job

citizen: a person who lives in a particular country and legally belongs to that country

civil rights: the rights that all people have in a society to equal treatment and equal opportunities

committee: a group of people who meet to make decisions or plans for a larger group or organization that they represent

constituents: people who live in a politician's area, state, or country

Constitution: a written document explaining the rules of a government or other organization

elected: voted into a job

frontiersman: a person who lives on unsettled land and hunts wildlife

NASA: the National Aeronautics and Space Administration, an organization that studies and explores space

Senate: the smaller upper house of the U.S. Congress

taxes: an amount of money that people pay to the government so that it can pay for public services

Index

LIGHTBOX

SUPPLEMENTARY RESOURCES

Click on the plus icon found in the bottom left corner of each spread to open additional teacher resources.

- Download and print the book's quizzes and activities
- Access curriculum correlations
- Explore additional web applications that enhance the Lightbox experience

LIGHTBOX DIGITAL TITLES
Packed full of integrated media

VIDEOS

INTERACTIVE MAPS

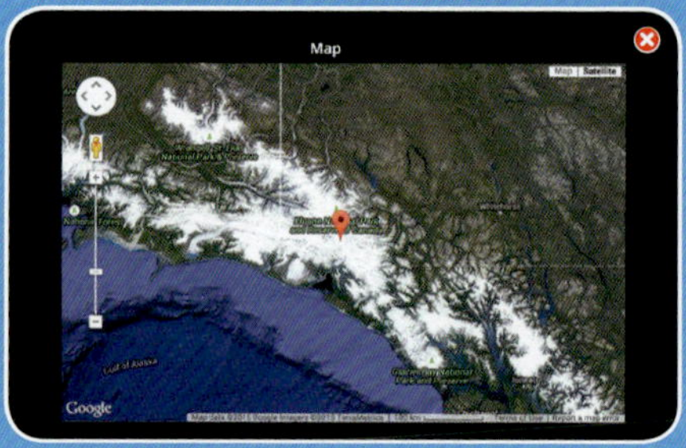

WEBLINKS

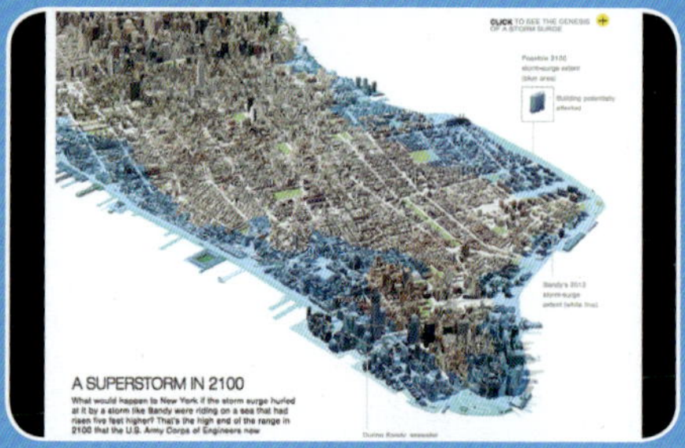

SLIDESHOWS

QUIZZES

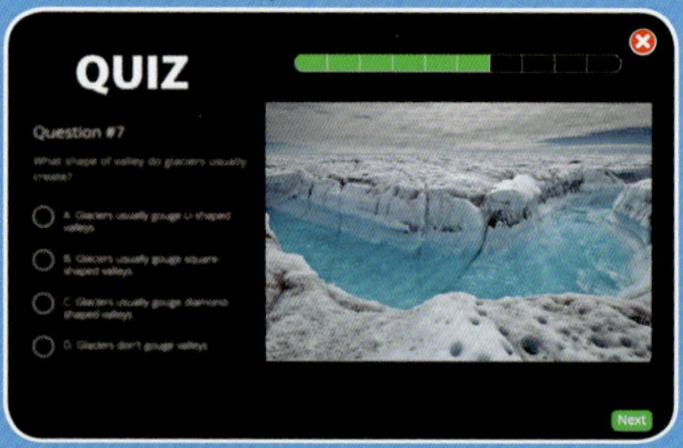

OPTIMIZED FOR

- ✓ TABLETS
- ✓ WHITEBOARDS
- ✓ COMPUTERS
- ✓ AND MUCH MORE!

Published by Smartbook Media Inc.
14 Penn Plaza 9th Floor
New York, NY 10122
Website: www.openlightbox.com

Library of Congress Control Number: 2020938423

ISBN 978-1-5105-5454-2 (hardcover)
ISBN 978-1-5105-5455-9 (multi-user eBook)

Printed in Guangzhou, China
1 2 3 4 5 6 7 8 9 0 24 23 22 21 20

062020
111019

Project Coordinator Heather Kissock
Designer Ana María Vidal

Photo Credits
Every reasonable effort has been made to trace ownership and to obtain permission to reprint copyright material. The publisher would be pleased to have any errors or omissions brought to its attention so that they may be corrected in subsequent printings. The publisher acknowledges Alamy, Getty Images, and iStock as its primary image suppliers for this title.